PRAISE FOR *SUPERBLOOM*

"In its intricately-patterned braiding of meditations on love, loss, everyday happiness and profound grief, Catherine Esposito Prescott's *Superbloom* is one of the most courageous and moving books of poems I've read in years. Employing ordinary language to reach beyond the ordinary into the realms of elegy and prayer, these poems evoke a kind of transformation, allowing us to glimpse that place where grief opens to the possibility if not the realization of miracle. At their core, these are hymns of gratitude: 'My heart is dust,' Esposito Prescott writes, 'but nothing is unbeautiful here.'"

—Michael Hettich
Author of *A Sharper Silence*

"Written during a year of seismic transformation, Catherine Esposito Prescott's poems are studies in patience and grace— poems that ask how the human spirit continues, the 'updraft of it, in the reel and pull of it,' and how love reshapes what remains. These poems, lush, lyrical, and fiercely tender, transform grief into an art of awareness, a 'theater of hope.' Catherine's is the voice of a confidant, talking truths and what-ifs. Between science and religion, is another wisdom, one of a mother. Beautiful and brutal and sawing and singing, these poems brought me to my knees."

—Alexandra Lytton Regalado
Author of *Relinquenda: Poems* (National Poetry Series)

Superbloom

Published by Gunpowder Press
Edited by David Starkey and Chryss Yost
PO Box 60035
Santa Barbara, CA 93160-0035

Front cover image by Scott Webb (Unsplash)
Author photo by Chantal Lawrie

ISBN-13: 978-1-957062-27-3
Library of Congress Control Number: 2025925283

www.gunpowderpress.com

Gunpowder Press is part of Gunpowder Poetry, a 501(c)(3) nonprofit
literary organization.

Superbloom

POEMS

CATHERINE ESPOSITO PRESCOTT

GUNPOWDER PRESS • SANTA BARBARA
2026

for Austen
(2005-2023)

Contents

3.

But listen to the voice of the wind
and the ceaseless message that forms itself out of silence.
It is murmuring toward you now from those who died young.

—Rainer Maria Rilke

1.

Become an alchemist. Transmute base metal into gold,
suffering into consciousness, disaster into enlightenment.

—Eckhart Tolle

Meditation on Blue

The shortest of the wavelengths, the highest
energy, always your favorite.
Sky and sea but not your eyes, not mine.
Not the melancholy, though tied to that.
Not even the heaviest grief, though anchored
in that difficult water. More the flow of liquid
through veins, unoxidized, unexposed, pure.
More the pea flower that turns boiling water
ultraviolet blue, then shifts to hot pink
when a drop of citrus is added. More the bell.
More shimmering, more lustrous. More
the backdrop for clouds, and their alphabet-soup
shapes, hieroglyphics of the air. Between
violet and cyan, visible, bright, you. Between
thought and memory, between the field
of energy we call the heart space, crocheted
into it. More the horizon, more
the Earth's halo, more strata of mountains,
more sublayer of sea. And let us not forget
delphiniums and morning glories. Let us not
forget your first words, the way your eyes
opened each day for us, the way the world
entered, the way your laugh entered us.
The rare M&M in the bag, the grape-flavored
lollipop. The berries we picked each summer
in the field at the farm on top of the mountain
from which we could see the mountains
that border our lake. In one photo, you hold
the berry between tiny toddler fingers up
to one eye, and the berry is bigger

than the orb through which life revealed
itself to you. In another, the berry juice
paints your face from ear to ear—.
and the joy feasting on sweet blue. The sapphire
of the sea we explored by ferryboat, the ultra-
marine, the lapis. Domes of churches, saintly robes.
If truth had a color, this would be it. A shade
less than shady. Improbable skin of the gods
who are ether. You now. You now. Moved
from this world to the next. Moved from skin
and bones to pure energy. Cobalt and indigo, and primary.
You, your place, in this realm, in the next one.
More teal where we live, and home to morphos
and borage flowers, which scale any scaffold
and taste like cucumbers, also favorites of yours.
At your celebration, a cache of dried forget-me-nots
blew into the sand, smaller than tears swept
from an eye. Into the earth, I heard you say,
let the ocean take it, let it wash away. There's nothing
left to hold onto. Never was. Though I felt it,
though I thought I could, though I believed
you were mine. Though I borrowed you. Though
we borrowed each other. Though we own nothing.

When on Earth

Santa Marta, Colombia, 2022

My eyes follow the swallowtail
paragliding over green palm fronds
as long as a newborn's body
in a bassinet. They curtain the forest,

create spaces where our breath cools, lungs
lift and expand without effort. My ears
see the foreign music of tropical
birdsong, an ecstatic sea of sound

on the edge of familiar. I come to
it the way a child draws to her mother's
tongue. I crave layers of green, crave the blue
above and below. Truth snaps into my

body like a forgotten lullaby, and
my heart sprints like a dog cut from her leash.

Diffuse and Intrinsic

If only it were a headache
If only the heat lifted in September
If only nothing
If only boredom
If only waiting was all we ever had to do
If only the rage could be tamed
If only the dragon were a rabbit
If only bats still scooped the air at dusk
If only I could sit upright, be pleasant
If only the storm were a breeze, light-scented, candle-ready
If only feminine energy were un-modest, if only the spirit-level were level
If only the surgeon could rob a bank instead of this body
If only the narrative could cure itself
If only he lived in reverse
If only dimples
If only laughter If only laughter If only laughter
If only proof of the veil lifting like a kimono over a pond holding the
        fullest moon
If only he didn't walk sideways, vision off-kilter
If only he never slurred
If only a flash weren't a strobe
If only we could trick time, turn the conversation
If only we could say *handsome* instead of *health*
If only the floor was marbled with the footprints left from dancing
We are lousy and sweet and unequipped for this
Oh boy, my boy, we are looking inside your brain, a shaken skull, the
        snowglobe shards splintered
We are reading the years of hits taken, of pain ignored like tea leaves
We are reckoning
I am wrecked

Field of Vision

Grand Canyon National Park, Arizona, 2021

The kids stand on the canyon's lip,
three living statues, two with earbuds, one too
young to drown out her parents'

voices. The one I want to bring into focus,
however, is the boy who would feel tremors
of headaches the following spring.

In this photo he wears a bemused smile
before turning to face the expanse, the wideness,
the stratifications of minerals and rocks and time,

millenia carved, fossils etched into what we
believe to be solid matter, stoic, barely yielding
to change, but now we know better

don't we—how organisms work
in concert, how every living thing needs
a host, and how cells choose to work

for the invaders rather than the native
body. And how one wrong move
can cause the body's programming

to go so tragically wrong. In the next photo
this parent-distanced teen, the one we are laser-
focused on, holds up his iPhone

to the canyon as if toasting it, impressed
by its long emptiness, its difficult distances
through which his voice could not travel.

I understand. It was all his eye could hold;
when I looked into the chasm, my visual field
became towers and spires named for Hindu deities,

and Indigenous deities—more myth than fact,
the origins complex and unknown. Farther,
sinuous stone shaped by water unremembered—

each layer an historical record of a sea
and a tide that once moved through this space,
an art piece—collage of rust, rose, gold,

and lavender with tufts of emerald.
Eighteen months later, his
expiration date was given—

eighteen years, during which time sped
and dragged and elapsed, then collapsed.
And yet today, when I open my Photos app

he is here standing on the rim of the canyon
taking a photo of the last world wonder
he would visit, but we didn't know

it then. All we knew was that his teenage
brain stopped to take it all in, and he marveled
in his way as he Snapped his friends.

Weeks after he left the body, I laid
on a healer's table and drifted to an alpine
wilderness with technicolor grass,

fluorescent flowers, a sky too blue
for this world. The boy who once stood
on the edge of the canyon sat on a mountaintop

in meditative silence. I didn't know
what to make of this journey, dear readers,
but I saw myself, a blue light, crawl

back into my body, and as I woke
I understood the way the rocks feel all beings
who have passed through their layers,

that even though the boy was all my eyes
could hold, the joy and the wonder
in my frame, it was his time, not mine.

Dear Soldiers,

Some bark is medicinal—
quinine, oak, willow—
for fever, spasms of pain,
one lick can freeze the mind,
transforming it from violent
to violet. What if this
could happen in landscape—
fields of war into fields of peace?
My work is a theater of hope.
I trace battlefields searching
for you, my brothers—
from grassy expanses
to the trees you climbed
before the furor of war burned
through you. Following the paths
of owls, you angle
your lithe bodies onto birch
limbs scaling toward all
you can see, while I peel
bark in sheets to write letters
you will not
live to read.

Fallen Poem

We didn't let your body linger
when the masonry gave out. We didn't wait
or wail, having seen your
spirit set free. The physical workhorse
of your body-turned-ash now feeds
soil under a giant white oak.
We will never say *quit*.
We will never say *lost*.
We won't even say *gave out*.
We say, *you are alive but unseen,*
beyond the five senses,
no longer bound to Earth,
though still to us. I feel
I could blink and see you
and know your current
curriculum. No longer subject
to rain, to cold, no longer lingering
in a tranquilized body, no longer
wrestling with the end of your life
when your life
was just beginning.

Leaving Home

Rocky Mountain National Park, Colorado, 2021

We ride up the side of the mountain.
My legs straddle Bingo, my daughter's

cling to Cocoa. Our workhorses canter,
swaying our bodies like lamps on a ship

in a storm-filled sea. Purple mountains
circle us like fatigue under the eyes, and the sky

sings, its blue like the inside of a god's
mouth. We sold the house we raised her in,

and now wander the earth like bourgeois
vagabonds. What does she think of home?

My daughter's mind is a vaulted ceiling,
maybe a heaven filled with Pegasus unicorns.

Mine is a stack of paper, torn maps, an infinite
scroll of words. We trace the perimeter

between house and house, childhood and adolescence.
My place in her life rotates. Today, I'm in front.

I am the scythe and the breadcrumb. Tomorrow
I'll be a swath of grass along her path. Our home

is more than a concrete foundation stuffed
with boxes of books and photographs, and china

from my husband's great aunt, crystal port
glasses from my grandmother, yet I have no

idea what my daughter will inherit,
and although I pack the boxes, it is not up to me.

The bend up ahead beckons, a crooked neck,
a crescent marking the trail. Her horse stops

every two minutes to feast on sweet, yellow grass.
Mine doesn't like the pull of reins on skin.

With a teenager's gait, she moves faster
when I pull up, when I offer anything

like resistance. I feel my breath rise
and lock in my chest, my lungs unable

or unwilling to let it go, ball or beast,
breath chained like an anchor attached

to no boat, with no spear, no net.
I know how this goes. I have backpacked

through dozens of countries, savoring languages.
I have sought what I needed from the world,

and so will she. My daughter rides alongside
a dusty-jeaned cowboy who tries to distract her horse

from stopping for another lick of grass.
The trail is thin, and the woods start to fold in.

The tops of trees touch like fingers of thinking hands,
an archway of green. My horse pauses.

The mountains are jagged, sloping. To look directly
at them is enough. Today, I want to see the world

only for what it is. How it ends: I watch
my daughter's copper hair catch

the sun. The cowboy gives his horse one
hard kick. They tear through the field.

The Swimmer

So she swam across   the sea,
      one woman   a boat
meters ahead   another behind
     and drones like judges
following   waiting   for her throat
     to burn, for her to choke
on saltwater.   Her job
     pressed   on
as spandex   imprinted
     her body   tattooing
its surface   like a leash
     held too tight   around
a dog's neck.   Why this hunger?
     I could say, it had something
to do with shame,   the tightrope
     women walk   between
metal and fire.   I could say
     her desire   rang like an alarm
drilling her body   blurring
     millenia-held beliefs
of never   enough.   Uncaged
among   starfish   among sharks
     like this   she razed   she erased
her mind   made a hollow   a fallow
     field   which begged—
no,   which dared
     a harvest   to rise

Fallen Poem

[after putting my cell

    phone face down

        my eye is drawn

            into] a halo of moon

      a ring a globe of light

    enters the sky

the moon and her moon

    a pageant of orbs

        their ebbs and illusions

            call our bodies to meet

        in a sky of dark turquoise

    sky of the deep sea

moon swims on the surface

    of water like bioluminescent

        beings in the open

            sea gradations

        of black and green

    where [everything is revealed]

the deeper our time

    whether or not the heart

        the mind in every cell

            is prepared to see

        (the laugh the gaze

    of someone who loves you

when he lets slip the look

    that's yours only)

        more colors emerge

            rose and lavender

        tonight let's circle the moon

    let's trace the arcs

to notice

    how light how absence

        how phosphorescence

            finds us

        like sugar cubes

    rubbed together

in the dark

Meditation on Worry

What petty tyrant lives in the skull's
black box, what erratic wavelengths
does it send, knife-sharpened, vertiginous,
spinning the mind, sowing rows

of discord, a ferocious music? There's plenty
for everyone in this wilderness,
in this squall of information—from quip
to CT scan, from sneeze to snore.

I'd rather sleep on a plethora of thorns,
on a bed that gives no rest than cancel
joy, even in the middle of doubt,
even if fear lances every thought,

coloring them in with the striated grays of clouds,
a children's book drawn with miserable art.

Tumor Reimagined

The tumor is a squatter.
The tumor, like cockroaches behind the wall.
The tumor disguises itself, throws a cozy wool blanket over its sharp hair.
The tumor is a survivalist. It thrives on dehydrated meals, on ammunition.
The tumor has all of the ammunition.
The tumor has its own zip code.
The tumor has its own genetic code.
The tumor has a name and a mutation. It has letters and numbers.
The tumor reinvents itself constantly.
The tumor has nine lives.
The tumor will die, will go to tumor jail, then rehab itself.
The tumor has its own rehab center.
The tumor has its own redemption narrative.
And the boy it has taken.
And the boy's brain like a hermit crab's shell
will ache and swell at the base
and it will crack
and we will crack.
And it will swell in pain.
And we will swell in pain.
And every function will fall prey
as grief stirs us into meditation paths,
as sand grits our socks, as it cuts into our feet.
The pain will not offset enough
for the pain is deep, the swelling is deep.
The tumor is stringing up a hammock and fairy lights.
The tumor is putting up photos now of itself—one month, two months, a baby.
And the boy feels the tape sticking to his brain stem,
gluing healthy cells together until they are oxygen-
starved seeds ripped of their coding, robbed
of their function to absorb the world through his senses,
to translate it, and to hold it before him a beautiful, fixable thing,
a map for his mind to draw itself onto.

Numb

The day we canceled joy—no, the day
we were told words we could not digest:
incurable, inoperable, palliative, the congestion
in our minds pitched rational thought
cliffside, and we left reason. This is not to say
we abandoned it like a newborn in a Moses basket
downriver. Let's just say it was swept
from us under tides of emotions. The sideways question
was: Would our son die before his birthday, before
the number we tied to adulthood, and a kind
of leaving anyway? An octopus lives for three to five years
in the wild. Our son, who called steak "snake"
as a young boy, lived five octopus lifetimes—or three
depending on the math. His spark, his spirit, his
whatever *it* is survives even longer as does the pain
of not seeing him. We have yet to cancel
his driver's license, his voter's registration.
Sages say death is a passing of form, from
not-so-solid matter to ether or a substance we
cannot sense, and therefore cannot name. Even
so, the worst is the tent of pain, a container,
a shadow that follows us, a cloak which blocks
us from seeing beyond it to anything close
to Rumi's field, toward any place where
we could pitch our gaze toward the divine. What is
one life but a borrowing, but lent time—for my son,
an octopus, myself, crowds of us walking
through this liminal space, this moment, our hearts
worn canyons, eroded more now, filed
down to raw and digesting a pain
greater than any tonic, greater even
than our desire to numb.

Meditation on Grief

We're like torn flags.
It sits like a medicine ball on our chests.

Other than that...
there is no other than that.

Impossible Care Package

Acne oil, tea tree formula, because you never know who you might meet over there.

Blue hoodie, the one you left behind, the one I accidentally donated. Apologies. Birkenstocks, your first pair. Cloudwalking and more hippie-than-thou, you're ready. Beef jerky.

Care package, this. (Insert sheepishly-happy emoji.) Cookies, of course, homemade, not the vegan ones. Coffee cake, vegan. (You were always a curious contradiction.) Crystals. Are you into crystals now?

Dental floss and deodorant. (See acne).

Ear plugs. (Useful for you last year when the pressure in your head caused sound-induced nausea.)

Fake fur hoodie found in your stolen car. (Why not?! It's soft and warm, and I'm making things up anyway.) A frisbee for fun.

Gel for your hair, a Ganesha for the altar you may now keep. (I'm just guessing here.) Granola, of course.

Headphones, noise canceling. (See earplugs.)

Inkjet printer to use with your computer.

Jeans, a book of dad jokes from your sister, juggling balls.

Kites. At least one.

Laptop. All of the laptops—the gaming one, the school one. (These were also donated, given to your friend as you wished.)

Mountain bike, which is in California with your cousin as per your request. You didn't know how we'd get it there, but now—from your overarching vantage point—you do.

Notebooks, pens, index cards.

Oranges and grapefruits because they travel well...and you loved citrus. An octopus stuffie. (We all have one.)

Pants, sport pants, comfy pants, all the pants. Probiotics. Prosciutto, the first food you ate after the penultimate hospitalization. Your iPhone. (It's with your bestie as you wished. The account is still active, so

you can send and receive messages.) Potato chips and pretzels and
packages of salted nuts.

Qtips. (See acne.)

Razor and razor blades, a completely new shaving kit. A robe? Do you
need a robe?

Sneakers (also donated, sorry), soccer cleats (kept), socks, deflated soccer
ball, your slippers, a Shiva murti (Nataraja, the dancing Shiva for said
altar), a seed found on the beach.

Tee shirts, only soft ones. A toothbrush.

Underwear.

Vitamins.

Winter coat, wool socks, and gloves.

X-ray vision. No, wait, can you send me this one? (Insert winking emoji.)

Yo-yo for the year of deep love and impossible sadness, for the year we had
to hold it all, the weight of the unbearable, how you carried it with
grace. A tear for the unknown, how we held you, how we were held.

Zero. What you need now, what you ever needed, the little you asked for
while in the body. The postage is impossible to calculate, but I cannot
shake the catalog of your needs, the list that rewrote itself for the span
of your life. You left at a natural cleaving point, just on time, but too
soon, and you went too far for this motherbrain, for her animal heart.

The Ride

To enter is to admit loss, to pit beauty against
everything else, from draped banyan root to sky.

Even the cirrus clouds, painterly, feathered,
Even the neon sun once mistaken in myth

for a mango, all of it drained, and I
am restless with memory. Today, joy

is lopsided, diluted with sorrow. And how
could it be otherwise? The rishis say

death is an illusion. Birth is a death, and
death is a birth, and I believe them.

Even though pierced with pain when our boy
left his body. Even though his lustrous presence.

Even the gift of his life. Even his peaceful end
as we sang "blackbird fly, blackbird fly." Even

as the future swung open its threatening door.
How do we? How can we? The eaves

channel rainwater down the sides
of our house. The rocks below glow

green with mold. Basil seedlings shout
through the soil. My heart is dust,

but nothing is unbeautiful here.
Although drained, even us. I ride my bike

miles into swampland, alongside the coast—
land of low brush, of saw palmetto and coontie,

fresh springs of clear water on one side of the path,
while landfills and garbage mark the other.

And it is always like this. Many miles in,
it merges into a collage I can almost make sense of,

a swirl of love and loss, pain and triumph.
The cacophony then ceases as my muscles

give way to pain, my body surrenders,
and my heart finds an opening,

then cyan, baby, turquoise, aqua, royal
come calling, a marvel, the many shades of blue.

2.

This is what it means to create: not to make something out of nothing, but to make order out of chaos.

—Harold S. Kushner

Touch

The delphiniums are up, the heart
flings itself wide. O buttercup. O rose.
The garden of gold stamens resists sleep.
Wild strawberries wink under greenleaf shutters.

White flowers cover their crowns like eyes—
the patch a many-headed goddess startled
awake, her seasonal sleep again denied.
Blue skies carpet the atmosphere, where

clouds travel like dandelion puffs.
It is too much. A casual frog crosses
the driveway, a bumblebee stuffs
its head into a trumpet flower, and ladybugs

tattoo my forearms. Sunlight spreads
as if from a broken bottle. I want to touch everything.

Home

Where the heart labors and lives;
where ripe mangos fall from trees;
where possums and raccoons scratch three lines in the ripest fruit;
where my nose follows the curve of a guava tree branch
inhaling an intoxicating perfume of sweet and fresh and hope;
where waves froth, churning plastic bags and broken shells onto shore;
where needlefish excavate the seabed;
where tourists turns shades of pink and brown;
where sun blasts memory, overrides, dizzying the mind, blinds;
where we are misled, where we are helped;
where we sleep, eat, and fuck; where we die;
where we write poems, where we study;
where our eyes climb entangled trunks of a banyan tree;
where we find sacred space in its branches;
where we find the sacred;
where we sit and gather;
where we are sent;
in what we choose, in what is chosen for us;
in the symbolic wing expanse of an osprey;
in the pointed direction of a steeple;
where messages are holy; where we are divine;
where we are calm; where we are restless;
in deep truth and in tinted lies;
in the bomb detonated, in the bomb transmuted
into cookstoves, into housing for coral;
in the mind's diary, in its insistent seeing;
in what we inherit; in what we donate;
in every discovery, in every dead end;
in every nest, every beginning,
every coming together of playground debris and twigs

to the seat you make; to what you make;
to the making; to generating
to the motor, the spark, the rays of ideas
filtered through consciousness;
in the coming and, especially, in the going;
where we find ourselves;
wherever we find ourselves.

Spirit Animal

The sloth was never your spirit animal
until it was. Once vibrant, once running
to scale lake-mountain trails, once streaking
down the soccer field, once never home.

Your future crawled by you in cap and gown,
the pomp never suited you, but that path
also. The tumor erupted enveloping healthy
brain cells. My love, the future, yours

surrendered itself. So the sloth. He sleeps,
he breathes, and by breathing knows he's living. So
the dynamic exchange of oxygen and carbon
danced in you, animated your listless life,

but only for one year. Then the branch broke,
then we lumbered, then we lived upside down.

What to Say When a Mom Asks If His Diet Caused It

Nothing is caused by nothing.

In fact, this big something was certainly
caused by something, but certainly it wasn't

that mango he ate at perfect sweetness
minutes before rot set in. It was nothing

we placed on the table, no chicken cutlets,
no capicola, salami, prosciutto, no wicked

cheese browned on pizza, no bacon crisp.
Occasional fast food was hardly prescient.

Neither hunger unmet. The boy became a boy
with no future, no choice but in how much to suffer.

Once, after radiation, we told our son to order
whatever he wanted for lunch and as much

of it as he wanted. That's when he knew
and we knew. That's when all budgets

disintegrated and our balance sheet shifted
to his happiness, his endurance. That day,

he ordered four entrees from his favorite ramen
restaurant: bowls of noodles and soup, fried

pork gyozas, and steamed shrimp dumplings.
It was his win—to savor every combination

of fat and sweet and spice knowing
this pleasure would be the last to leave

as the invaders claimed his brain, then his
body, spreading like brush fire to a wild rage

no wind could enter, no water blow out.

Fallen Poem

At the top there's drama
below the abacus and the cane
                                        a world tilts, spins into
an open hand.   A tent flap door unfolds.   Beyond clock-time   a rainbow,
                        in the lea, downward facing, bleats a lonely sheep

+
                        An upside-down tent
crescent moon holding dark sky   the upturned apple
fish angle for deeper seas   in time
                  the arrow points down   to the letter "L" (almost midway).
                  a die is thrown   open your eyes

+
                                        A crescent moon lays on its side.
A fish changes direction.   Whose cell phone rings?
    The fountain splashes sideways,

the view from headstand,   speech bubbles rising in unread breaths.
An airplane makes its descent.

Baby turtles struggle toward the ocean—
                        the pull of home, a magnet.

+
Bemused
            was the sheep
                  when a bee tried to startle its quiet.
                        Like placing a cane in an open palm.
            Lightbulbs were once considered miracles
as were flowers   as were shooting stars.
    Trees, too, if you believe me.

+

He sits in a canted tower
with a useless magic wand   a baby turtle shuttling back toward land.

The key opens to   a flashlight beaming upward
Dramatic masks are uncalled for;
        the clock ticks for everyone   right and left.
Balance your scales.

No Words

I don't know how to find that place inside
where every chamber and hollow fills with grace.
Today, my tongue is a rainbow tied

to a rock, held, contracted. My wide
heart's got a kink, and I can't trace
back to the original crease; even though inside

flushes with blood, the violet arteries ride,
form a tree with branches, filled with lace
that grows and flows through me, today's tide

rushes in the way toxins do up the open side,
through the tear, the orifice, the agape face.
Today's news deadens the anima from the inside.

I don't know how to stand, star-studded, wide-eyed,
to seek the mystery of how a mango finds space
to grow, how (though heavy) it holds on to the tree. I've tried

to meditate, to sit in silence, but my thoughts hide
in sorrow. My pen is a racehorse pacing.
I don't know how to find that place inside.
Today, my tongue is a rainbow tied.

My Body Resigns

The marksman laces a target
into his vision like my mother threads
her quilting needle; he points his bow,
unsilences his gun. I am in the center;
no, my body is centered, though erring,
lilting in its thoughts from left to right,
from earth to cosmos; my body,
a dancing diary, a bluster of cells;
how it has bled for years, how it has served;
how punished for the apple I offered,
for the pomegranate I ate; for the lives
I've birthed, for the hundreds more I've denied;
for the divine light and lack thereof;
for the answers it gives; holy/unholy;
especially its wisdom screaming
from my opened-and-closed hips;
especially its solitude-dreams;
this is how women are veiled; how disappeared
how silenced; we who sow and sing and sew,
we who kindle words to fire;
denied our hunger, we are massaged,
we are messaged; as they cock their triggers,
we hobble; we fall and call it nesting;
we brace our bodies while gathering
food for the hunters; we miracle nothing to plenty;
we who create feast after feast;
who do all the holding, are never held.

Lens

Redwood National Park, California, 2022

We passed through a cathedral of redwoods.
Sunlight split the canopy
like light through splintered
stained glass. Though I do
not believe in many gods,
though I am not welcome
in many houses of worship.
though I am not considered
whole by many religions,
I laid my body down.

My daughter lifted her arms and spun
like a carnival ride, swirling
her magenta raincoat
against the understated
palette of northern
California forest.

*Take a picture
of all of this*, she commanded
as she twirled.
Impossible, I answered,
then widened my lens as far
as it would go.

Laughing with You

is a helium lift,
two hundred pounds

of nylon expanding
as we rise over

tea-party houses,
quilted fields;

a quick charge,
piano chords

sounding through water
as molecules swim

into kaleidoscopic
shapes; if not love,

it's yeast finding its flour,
the engine its rev;

sun punches through clouds,
light needles into my blood;

the boundary of you
makes out with the boundary of me;

I become the field,
become the sea

Meditation on Red

Anger is too easy, too expected.
Also, young cheeks blushing
with new love or caught
in 30-degree air on a winter
morning at the bus stop.
Red is heat, and its absence.
It's all we know—and its opposite.
Sometimes sunrise, and when
sunset, a sailor's delight. More
than one war god. More than one
planet. A furious, famous spot.
Monthly reminder. Not envy.
Jealousy, sometimes. cosmic dust
and laser beams. Night vision,
celebration, courage, sacrifice,
and war after war. Of course, blood.
Of course, the heart. The longest
of lightwaves, the longest of grudges,
the unending list of unmet needs.
Associated with house, home, hearth,
nest and all of its implications,
it is survival, which comes in many
hues and primary and the first
color babies see after black
and white, the first step beyond
binary, our entry color to the full-
chromatic index, the coveted 64-
color crayon box. Red hots,
cinnamon dots, peppermint drops.
Mouth and tongue and lips.

And a hot head, and the hair
of under two percent of the population,
which includes my daughter,
and not me. Also acne. And dominant.
And aggressive. Also not me.
Roses, if we're going there.
Peonies, poppies, almost,
pouty tulips, the amaryllis, more-
exotic hibiscus and roselle,
where we source bloom-red tea.
And let's not forget the antioxidant
parade: apples, cherries, strawberries,
raspberries, litanies of tomatoes,
pomegranates, the first forbidden fruit.
When you cut one, juice squirts
directly into your eyes, spray-
paints the counter and your clothes
deep magenta. Inside, a trove
of rubies shine like healthy ovaries
enlarged one-million percent. Cases
of seeds suspended in liquid
like a national guard with no country—
the cells that begin all life, the invisible
ones that hold all of our ache, our yearning.

Rash

Concentric interlaced circles, pink, like the wintermints my grandfather
kept in the car. Chalky, candy-but-not-candy buttons. Covered in
constellated red pin pricks and large, raised welts orbiting his torso. We
had never seen skin turn on itself as we did when our world knitted to
experimental pills taken down with water—one for chemo, one for nausea,
one for anxiety, one for sleep. Spreadsheets of pill schedules. No wasted
time. No wasted space that year. Also, no lipstick stain on his neck. No
prom. No graduation. No sugar. No jewels. To die young is either an act of
grace or a punishment or neither. They die like old men but in record time.
My father-in-law played the part of a dying man for two years until his body
no longer stayed upright to gaze at the desert mountain beyond his living
room. He ate steak and cursed his handlers. Then, he left his body, released
the mountain, gave up the horse. My son turned to strawberries in his final
months—the red and sweet of them—until he could no longer swallow.
My grandmother ate coffee cake by the sheet. Now I see death as a pause,
a caesura, in the narrative, a change of courses at the table. The medium
says my son is strong on the other side, his skin clear, muscles returned.
Why would I not believe her? As he transitioned, I saw him go, I saw his
happiness, his skin olive again, his abs in place. No doctor could confirm or
deny when I said he was leaving his body and returning and leaving again
for days. They left me to my madness knowing there was no pearl forming
from this grit, no world in which our pain could be soothed by a caretaker's
voice, the right pills, mints under the tongue.

Meditation on Beauty

My eyes can't see the writing on the wall,
even the one I mortared,
my hands wrapped in cement.

Women don't build walls,
they scale them,
they heal them
they birth wall breakers.

This city passes over
my un-Botoxed face.
The city does not want to read
a woman's lifelines.

Some days I want to lie down
in the street, my eyes climbing tree crowns,
tracing every shard
of sunlight
hitting the ground.

My friends want better masks—
new noses, new eyelids,
blank-page faces.

A woman alone
is a dangerous thing—
idle hands
belonging to no god,
no devil.

I cannot fix myself
nor my friends
nor the wall.

Beauty finds me
in silence
in a mridanga drumming,
fills my ears with a pulse
pulled from a seed sound
older than the void,
older than the universe itself.

Fallen Poem

When the world cracks open
when a blip in time brushes
its stiff bristles against your life,
the one of love and genius,
the one with many doors,
an empty blacktop you pave with calendar
entries. Plausible futures lean toward
degrees and more photos of smiling faces
shot in the afterglow of the timeline's
passage. How little you know.
It's not the candle's wick burning at both
ends, it's the wax itself, the marrow
of it, that burned to ether, the rough
fatigue, the fire burned with no wick
to hold it—scarred blacktop, scarred marrow.
Little upside-down life—beyond fallen, beyond
sorry—beyond lifeline and escape hatch.
Life of no tomorrow. I scavenged
language to make these poems. They
are what's left of the fire, they are the ashes
breathed into my skin and what
remains of our impossible year.

Rentals

The cardinal converses with me
from an anemic bamboo branch
his nest, a mess, a wonder.

I toast the tree that seems to die
but does not. Our house was
a backdrop, scenery.

Mountains fit like serrated
knives into the valley. This is home, too.
A rowboat suspended in a lake, too.

It is like this: an earring finds its resting
place inside a lobe. A mouth in the sweet
tundra of another mouth.

Decades ago, a colleague chanted
"Everything is temporary!"
every time he crossed Fifth Avenue.

Storefronts glittered with designer
sunglasses, hundred-dollar journals
wrapped in silk. I wanted it all,

not to wear, not to own, but to have something
to weigh me to this earth.
I made a home out of collected things:

the matchbox from Morocco,
a postcard from Capri,
Neruda's dreamlike poem drawn onto the wall,

his words a home, home as analog,
analogy, home as a gathering
of all I could never hold.

Quantum

Waiting for the moon to swallow
the sun, years ago, we watched

with the patience of preschoolers
for what some may have thought

was the end of the world.
The end of light—even for a second—

terrifies us. But as we came to find,
it was not the end at all, but a passing

through as when friends meet
along the path, exchange hellos,

maybe an anecdote, a refrain of a well-
loved song, and then move on.

Every time I thought the world might
end, it hasn't. My world. Our world.

As in when you left it. As when our sun
fell from the earth. As when pain electrified,

lightning struck every nerve, even
then the world did not end. What if you

exited stage left only to find another stage?
When the soccer mom envisioned

you crossing Biscayne Boulevard,
then turning to her car and waving

as if signing off, what if you walked towards
something as you left us. Out of sight,

and beyond what current science shows,
what if you walked into what we believed

to be shadow only to find nothing but light,
brightening and extending forever into itself?

3.

*Now is the time to expand your heart and find some love
for the universe and everything in it.*

—The Pattern app

Meditation on Yellow

The golden hour, the third in the spectrum,
and sunflowers, and bananas, and the sun,
the afterglow of its set and its rise,

and citrus, and clean and bright, gleaming
starshine, between green and orange, daffodils,
aspens in late autumn, leaves in decay, dying.

Also eternal, also indestructible, the skin
and the bones of some gods, certain stinging bees,
it commingles and communes well with purple.

Royal robes compliment gold, foolish
or not, the bright, shimmering disco ball, the city
of jewels, the ego's center, power and winning.

Every one an illusion. Every trophy, every minute
and monument. Every brocade, every chain.
The photos, the poses, all you possess, titles, too.

But the light of you, still here. Although earth
reclaimed your body, although carbon reunited with carbon.
Although your carbon feeds a tree, more limbs

than a human body could hold, and more carbon.
We write *gold*, and it autocorrects to *god*. We forget
the luster, the wonder beyond our senses, beyond

these words, even though they were brought to us
in one legend by the divine herself. What is my job
here, as a mother missing her son? There are no words

for a mother without her son—not widowed or widower,
not unmothered—beyond bereft, without, lacking, minus,
beyond bereaved, deprived of, dispossessed,

which implies layered suffering, lamentation, and left.
We know very well what I am missing. We have no
language for who I am, for what I may become.

Ginger Ice Cream

In the mid 90s, we entangled
with curries, elegiac about the slip
of a note from our hands. We read
and wandered and wondered about love.
When we realized it was all we had to do,
life seemed too easy and too hard.
When I fell, it was hard—iced-over
cement tore black tights, blued muscle;
the guy from the gallery became a fated affair,
an important actor in the story of my life
not unlike the ginger ice cream I searched
for in Chinatown one afternoon. After
slipping into a nameless storefront,
I pointed to the thing I wanted—a sweet,
spicy mound, not complicated, just milk,
heavy cream, sugar, eggs, and a thick
helping of ginger, its golden root fibrous—
beloved by many healers and seekers
but unbeknownst to me, a girl raised
in the shadow of New York City, a girl
filled with old curses, a habit of running
and hiding, and taking what was given
without question, for whom desire was
exotic, and unaffordable. Dreams
were labeled champagne taste
and our people stuck to a beer budget.
Back then, I didn't know how to divest
inheritance, but that afternoon
when the sweetness hit my tongue,
an ache sparked in me—a hunger

not for any one thing in particular,
certainly not ice cream—and my arms
reached around the world like a belt,
and I resolved to press the full force
of my body into this life.

Survival

Before the forsythia blooms, before its yellow stars
lobby heaven, before the kiss, before even the pleading,
another surgery, another gala, a royal cleaving.
No one gathers more soul swag, no one flies a higher
kite than the one singing, with a voice acrobatic

swinging through music scales. Bring on the Indian drums,
Panamanian flutes, American guitars, webs of sound,
arching for octaves, realms of mothers, of healers, of ecstatic
care, and of the deepest caves; this is how the heart survives
every eclipse, and how it returns, rocking and crooning its hello.

Meditation on Song

1.
This month marks the day
my daughter arrived,
fontanelle scooped and shallow,
a pool, a chasm pulsing
as her mind opened.

Her spirit gleaned
wicker furniture in the birthing
center, the first light of day
leaking through curtains.

My voice sang what a new mother sings
to her child, each note woven as a spell.

2.
In ancient times,
it was believed
that words called life
into existence,
sonic building
blocks created
the world
and sustained it.
Our work
was to praise
the energy
at the source
through sound.

3.
On the anniversary
of our birth,
and when we die,
people sing for us.
What else remains:
a lullaby to hush a crying baby,
a whine when we bite into a tart lemon,
a shriek when sharp air hits the lungs.

4.
In our last home, a mockingbird
met me each day. She lived
in a neighbor's bamboo,
perched on the highest stalk.
When I sang, she returned my song.
I don't know if she was instructing
me where to find breakfast
or if a storm was coming
or nothing so logical.
It was a hard year,
and I sang every day.
When I called out,
she answered,
both of us chanting
I am here. I am here.

Meditation on 35

Trees saged over us,
one-hundred years into their lifetimes,
carrying messages under soil.

My hair was pixie,
a short, spiked afterthought, my life,
the size of two small boys.

The kitchen table held rainbow-colored
plastic bowls filled with dried cereal,
raisins, goldfish. We ate too fast

for politeness, for linens. Hunger
dictated every move.
Between walking to the beach,

between what passed for school,
between afternoons at the children's museum
sorting fake food, processing

plastic oranges and learning to limbo,
between after-dinner dance
parties and swim lessons,

there was never silence. We gathered
mangos in a friend's yard. Trees rained
fruit to the tiny humans below.

Large, oval eggs, golden orbs
polka-dotted her lawn like many fallen suns.
The present moment focused

every thought. The boys' hands
gathered as many as they could carry.
We had no recipe to follow.

The world was as it is, as it's always been, 50
but our horizon focused on the forever-
summer sky. This was before grief,

before the myth of Icarus crystalized
in their minds, before many diagnoses.
The world was too new for sleep.

We peeled back the skin, and tossed
slivers of sweet fruit into our mouths.
Nectar poured from our lips soaking our feet.

Superbloom

Santa Barbara, CA, 2023

Striped rocks saddle the shoreline
of the park where sea rocks like long otters
or ancient watery tombs draped with grass
the color of something grown to its peak
before the rot. Let's call it defiant green,
the green of late teen years, of early 20s, young-
adult green. My sister surveys the rocks,
some laced with what looks like marble—
bright sashes of iridescent white—
some as if tanned a tawny brown, some
disfigured, open where water's incessant
push softened them, made them thin.
She doesn't know how to cross them. Most
surfaces curve into themselves or end
too soon, before a foot could fall, or have jagged peaks.
We are all working out how to get through.
Around us every green thing lifts a flower
thanks to the rain, which comes every day,
unseasonal, uninvited. I cannot remember
a time when I have cried more. We're searching
everywhere for a cure for Austen's cancer.
Scientists are breaking apart molecule
after molecule to see if one might be
the fighter cell we need it to be.
Around us, fog grows light. We are in it,
but poppies shout orange, the agave screams
its yellow flowers up toward an imaginary
sun. The grass no longer just grass, lemondrop
flowers dance on its breath. Even
the cliff holds tufts of heart-red flora.
Every living thing blooms bright as our hope.

Good Friday

Oleta River State Park, North Miami Beach, FL, 2023

We don't have to argue about evolution anymore,
or the degree of light from the late-afternoon sun
or whether we should order Cuban or Japanese
for dinner. I walk through the trails you once rode,
the trails you should be riding now. How am I here
and you are not? Scratch that. In the place
where your tires rolled over pine needles, I chase
the arc of your presence, the sway and switchback
of every turn, the unsmooth rocks under foot,
the branches of broken trees that are held
by other trees. Of course, the way you are held,
the way we are held. We don't need to argue anymore.
I do not fear death, but I don't want it—not mine, not yours,
of course never yours. When I thought of you,
just now a swallowtail danced on my shoulder.
When I think of you, when we visit each other,
I want no less than this. But today, let's stay here,
let's walk along the mangroves, catching
and finding our balance as we go.
We don't have to argue about anything anymore.
Let us know only words for love now,
only words for hope now. Walk with me
along the trail a little bit longer.
My navigator, I have no map.
My easy one, I'll carry you across every bridge.
I'll even remember to bring your walking stick,
and I'll carry it wherever you need to go.

We Used to Have More Time,

but now you live beyond it, beyond
time and space, so you have none
of it, or you have all of it. I'm not
sure how it works. Is it the kind

of thing that we see in sci-fi
plots, a prismatic kind of life
where everything blooms rife,
and all at once? Where you and I

are the same yet distinct, you
there, me, here. Where is *there*?
I think of you every hour. The air
around me becomes a perfume

of crushed rose and jasmine, attar
of grief—incense and burning
butter, and the tender musk
of you gone from this sphere.

Once, we believed in time, in its horizon.
Without you, my son, there is none.

Fight

With a yellow tube, a worm, a thick fishing line
strung from nose to throat, with suction,
with a maximum dose of dexamethasone,
with a morphine drip, with pause,
with the last experimental chemo
not working after the prior three,
with all avenues explored, with all trials
done and failed and done, with my son
done, though we failed to believe,
could not see it for this kind of love rips
open closed doors, and the end was as impossible
to conceive of as was the beginning, the unknown
so bright and terrifying. In the beginning,
when every doctor said he would die,
my son asked me what we believed came next,
and we spoke of energy and karma
and reincarnation and the words of every wisdom
tradition, which all speak of eternity,
and this eternal self—soul, puruṣa, ātman, spirit—
the unaccounted-for weight held in the body,
the part beyond the senses. He took mental
notes, and engaged every family member
as if taking a poll and assembling
a spreadsheet of afterlife possibilities,
as if by letting all the ideas into his consciousness
he might qualify for all. His senior thesis
esoteric and unprovable, yet mandatory
to show every sad-eyed doctor, every stoic
researcher, every tear-addled friend
who translated the diagnosis, who read

"universally fatal" and understood my son
would be part of that statistic. *Always*
an overachiever in the strangest things,
my mother said, as he graduated
from high school and Earth school.
With him so close to transitioning,
with bags packed, with a will tucked
in his iPhone, with humor in it,
with me and his father not in it,
with his soul beginning to leave his body,
he looked at the alphabet my husband drew
in lagoon-blue ink, and with a liberated
finger, one not laced to machines,
from the one hand unmonitored, untapped
for veins, he drifted to three letters,
four times, and signed, "away," meaning,
for me to go away, and maybe that he too
would be going, but in an opposite and unfollowable
direction. When he nodded that I understood,
I did what a mother does, and as I had done
countless times over 18 years. I kissed
and hugged him, and he did as he had done
for 18 years, lovingly shrugged me off
like a dog shaking water from its back,
or a hiker throwing down his pack,
as if to say like any teenager, *Enough, Mom.*
I've got it from here.

Enlightened, Exalted

are the exact words The Oracle uses to speak
of my son. They remove the sting
of his physical absence, which lives
in every cell, in every neuron, every quark—

from thought to emotion to exclamation
to the big nothing, which is what absence feels
like most days—the chasm, the missing piece that leaves
us reaching in shadow spaces for connection—

the signs of haunting, the way the sun spokes
through clouds just for us, the way we see
him goofing off on The Other Side as he
would on this side. As always, he jokes

with friends, grooves to rap and hip hop, scrolls
our world while surfing his own, ignoring our calls.

Fallen Poem

We are past the age of passionate responses
to political questions. My husband and I propose
nothing so much as *why* or *how*. We don't seek
answers. After the internationally renowned researcher said,
We may never know the cause, we took his words
and fed them to the fire with *what ifs*, with stalks of lavender,
holy basil, and lemongrass. Incense for the lost, for the light
we will always find ways to honor. Our home
now a temple to our lost son. Our backyard bonfires.
Our conversations quilt hope and resignation,
fight and release. The world is full of *and*, every thing
lives with its opposite. All of it held in the heart,
now so full, now so wrecked, it seems like a done-for thing.
But dying of a broken heart is cliché, and we refuse
its eroding, melancholy facade. Yes, grief is a kind of exile.
Yes, the pain lodges in muscle and bone, drenches every cell.
A week after my son passed, my legs seized with an ache
so deep as if I had walked a year without stopping,
every muscle spasmed and short-circuited. I asked him
to release the physical pain, to lift it from my body, and he did.
I understand how pain can fester, becoming its own
righteous convention. The pain. My pain. Our pain.
It becomes a pet that hops onto your seat, steals
your meatballs, and everything that could heal you.
My oh mine. We travel, we find new mountains
to climb, we move our bodies until we exhaust them.
In this, we expand our bandwidth. And the heart finds its way through
the debris and pushes us back into life.
And we—the hologram of us, the story we're creating
between end points—scramble up to the vista, and drink.

Rockstar Mom,

the one with all of her edges
blunted, points down, shaved;
the one with extra, splintered
tips; the jagged-edged star,
the rough star, the metallic-death star,
the star with no name, the star that's missing
a point, the star that is missing.
Where is the star? Where is the mom?
When the child dies, where does the mom go?
Is the mom in the star, is the child the star?
The Rockstar Mom is more rock than star,
more molten, more melted, more goo
at the center, more spinning,
and the spinning is, the spinning
is, the spinning is out of control,
the heart of the Rockstar
Mom is hot, is whirling, is boiling over,
without a center. The Rockstar Mom throws
herself into the sky in search of the child,
and the child is back to star, back to stardust,
back to the space between matter, back
to light, and the mom, the mom, the mom without
her rock, the mom without her star
must work beyond time to find him.

Fallen Poem

If I stepped on a scale right now,
I wouldn't weigh more than a feather.

The strength it takes to keep
my faith alive is no small thing.

Polaris seems closer than the dirt
undulating with worms & mycelium under my feet.

The unseen is within reach, and the seen
is light years from my grasp.

A temple, my mind, the simplest thoughts
fall through space—there's a lack

of gravity, a failure to hold,
a piece that's missing.

The Swamp

Everglades National Park, Florida, 2023

From sibilants, from stone, the sweetwater
of sense, of story, of language. From the zygote,

from the tribe, from the offhand glitter
of birth, of fate, you came. How could we reduce

your life to suffering? How could your story
end with pain? My love, when we speak of your life

let's make it a case study in yearning met, in your
superior sense of humor, your stampede of joy.

My dear, let's not limit your life to its end.
Let's carve the narrative arc to the time you slept

under the sky's matrix of stars with crocodiles,
egrets, and roseate spoonbills at the edge of Florida.

In the Ten Thousand Islands, you worked an oar,
evolved to navigate waterways without modern

tools—only with a compass and a map. You felt
hunger and learned how to add water and heat

to almost anything to end that desire.
You saw the pensive expanse of night,

and knew the ease of sleep among wild animals.
You knew you were part of something more vast

than one life would have you believe. Maybe
there were comets. I want to say the sky winked,

that you were let in on the great joke, and so you
knew which experiences had to be digested, which

could be discarded. I want to say you knew
how we've made a complicated mess of life,

and you pried your mind from the muck and saw
the play for what it is. In the unruly grass, at the edge

of the great swamp, sleeping atop a kayak, I hope
you knew it then: the futility, the love, even the arc.

What we choose and what chooses us. How, if lucky,
we carve a space in our clay lives for grace, for something

golden to weave through us, that binds us, holds us, then
lets us go. My love, the hardest thing we've ever had to do

was to say, *it's ok to leave us, you have suffered enough*.
When your suffering ended, ours began. We could not have

known every pothole on this road, every trap. We could
not have seen that remembering your exuberance

would be the only light worth navigating by, the only way
we could dare move through our craving to see you again.

The Beautiful Goodbye

In the beginning of my son's diagnosis,
I gathered bouquets of light—broken stars,
shards of lit bulbs, stems of sunlight,
and we feasted on them, on what shone
in his eyes and in ours, that shared spark,
that fire through the storm of medical
procedures and medicine and therapy
and devices and surgeries and palliative
this and that, and no-cure blah, blah, blah,
and the nascent research, and the mis-
understandings, and the lack of under-
standing, and the lack of funding, by which
I mean a cure had to yet to be funded,
had yet to be found, and so terminal,
and so random, and so no-cause the cancer
which would take my son's life,
and so bad-luck, and so lightning-strike
and so heavy the insurmountable
mountain that cast its foreboding shadow
over us, daring us to turn into exaggerated
monsters, the saddest ones, our faces contorted
and paralyzed in grief masks, even as we balanced
the unbearable weight among us. We held
this bouquet of light until the very end,
until infused with opioids and benzos,
and painfree and surrounded by love,
until enveloped in the ultimate hug,
in the updraft of it, in the reel and pull of it,
when his spirit left the body, when it whooshed
out of the crown of his head, and we knew

even after a week of not speaking, after
a week of leaving, he was gone. And this
is the crazy part, not that he died, which we
knew would happen, but how quiet the end was—
how after hours of chanting, after a minute
singing our lullaby, how his eyes waved open
and closed like two hands, palms signing off,
and how silent his last breath and the final
wave of his ribs as they lifted and sank,
and after a year of sickness and struggle, a year
of sadness and relentless hope and crazy love,
he flew to the next realm, and how we felt his flight—
and how quickly he went, how without protest,
how utterly faint, how without sound he lifted
and left, and how great the void, and how gentle the thrust.

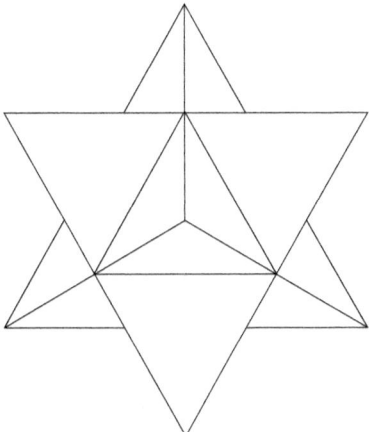

The Visitation

No, not gone. Not missing. O no, not gone.
You live in the tetrahedron's angles,

in the star's music, invested in memory.
You came to me with warm skin, full of breath,

of life returned, no longer emaciated, off-kilter,
no longer leaving this world, rather, coming

into it. You said you missed texting, and asked
to use your dad's phone. I remembered then

your laughter, the hard time you'd give me,
that snicker-click of tongue on the roof

of your mouth, sideways grin and glance,
and how you always reset me

like a typewriter carriage pulled to the left.
Though warm, though between stars, you

and our guides said it was time to head to IKEA,
so we jumped into an army-ready Land Rover

and drove up I-95. The road slipped into shadow,
moon rocks below where pavement used to be.

I saw the outline of a crocodile, the mane
of a horse crossing, a few unnameable beasts.

Rocks disappeared, and we floated. Still
in joy, I fell through darkness, and woke.

The look you mirrored onto my face, the warmth
of you settled into me as sunlight crossed the threshold.

So many suns we shared, my love. *You always
got me*, you told the medium, meaning I knew

your state of mind with one shared look. And you
always got me, my son. Still do. You know how

I love order, even the facsimile of it, even
a clearly-marked maze and labeled bins, even

my art of searching for meaning in chaos. It was
the only way to get me to return home,

to detach, as you'd say, to retrace the distance
between where you live now and us Earthside.

Memories bubble up inside of me, each a pocket
of joy, iridescent and light. They circle and pop,

circle and pop, filling the air around us
with quick bursts of rainbow and rain.

Here then elsewhere,
here then elsewhere

NOTES

"Diffuse and Intrinsic" – In September 2022, my son Austen was diagnosed with DIPG (diffuse intrinsic pontine glioma), a type of DMG (diffuse midline glioma)—a rare, pediatric brain cancer located in the brain stem.

"Dear Soldier" – Inspired by medicine used during the Civil War.

"Fallen Poem" – Many poems in this collection share the same title. Before Austen was diagnosed, I was playing around with randomness using word dice to create poems. After he died, I couldn't write at all. To start writing again, I would pour word tiles onto my dining room table and wrote poems around them. "The Swimmer" – for Diana Nyad, who, at 64, swam from Havana, Cuba to Key West, Florida.

"Fallen Poem" – An ekphrastic poem in conversation with "The Guiding Light," a painting by Harold Ancart, displayed at The Whitney Biennial in 2022.

"Tumor Reimagined" – DIPG is an aggressive tumor that affects the parts of the brain that control all vital bodily functions—from heart rate to chewing to swallowing to breathing. Austen's tumor had the H3 K27M mutation, which is less responsive to treatment.

"Numb" – Rumi: "Out beyond ideas of wrongdoing and rightdoing, / There is a field. I'll meet you there."

"The Ride" – The "myth" refers to the apocryphal story about the monkey god Hanuman. When young, Hanuman mistook the sun for a mango and swallowed it. // A rishi (ṛṣi) is an enlightened person or a super yogi. // "blackbird fly, blackbird fly" are from "Blackbird" by The Beatles.

"My Body Resigns" – Written in response to the the overturning of Roe v. Wade.

"Rash" – Austen went on a clinical trial which paired two medicines: ONC201 (which is now FDA approved) and Paxalisib. His body couldn't tolerate the high dose or the combination. The trial may or may not have extended his life.

"Quantum" – Written on April 8, 2024, the solar eclipse. // This poem was performed with the electro-pop duo Afrobeta and Miami Sound Space choir in collaboration with O, Miami at Vizcaya Museum and Gardens on October 30, 2024.

"Meditation on Song" – With gratitude to Dr. Katy Jane's lectures on the Vedas.

"Meditation on 35" – The mangoes were gathered in Jen Karetnick's yard.

"Superbloom" – When Austen was sick, I was invited by Chryss Yost and David Starkey (of Gunpowder Press) and Emma Trelles (then Poet Laureate of Santa Barbara) to give a reading in Santa Barbara. Austen insisted I go. I stayed less than 48 hours, and wrote this poem.

"Fight" – The overall survival rate for DIPG is nearly 0%.

"The Swamp" – Austen's high school sponsored a mandatory Outward Bound trip for freshman to the Ten Thousand Islands in the Everglades. Although covered in mosquito bites when he returned, he said he never slept better.

"The Visitation" – Thank you to Caridad Moro-Gronlier and O, Miami for producing the Poetry Tarot workshop at the historic Deering Estate in Miami in April 2024. That night, I drew the King of Pentacles, which often refers to a person and is sometimes associated with spiritual attunement. Looking at the card triggered the memory of a strange dream, then a realization. The song "Samurai Cop" by Dave Matthews Band played in my mind immediately after the poem came out. Briefly, "(Oh Joy Begin)" was included in the title. Thank you for the visit, kiddo.

Acknowledgements & Gratitude

Thank you to the editors and staff of the publications which first published these poems:

American Poetry Review: "What To Say When A Mom Asks If His Diet Caused It"

Colorado Review: "The Swamp," "Superbloom," "The Ride," "Fallen Poem," and "Fight"

Josephine Quarterly: "Meditation on 35"

NELLE: "Good Friday" and "Rockstar Mom,"

Painted Bride Quarterly: "Numb," "The Visitation," and "The Beautiful Goodbye"

Poets Reading the News: "My Body Resigns"

Tahoma Literary Review: "Spirit Animal"

+

Deep gratitude for the early readers of this collection, Mary Block, Jen Karetnick, and Caridad Moro-Gronlier; for my writing community, my SWWIM Editors—Mary Block, Jen Karetnick, Mia Leonin, Caridad Moro-Gronlier, and Alexandra Lytton Regalado—and the Poetas: SWWIM Team + Elisa Albo, Rita Maria Martinez, and Emma Trelles—and my writing group, the Matrix, who were the first responders to many of these poems, Felice Belle, Nicole Callihan, Brenda Cárdenas, Kai Coggin, Jane Creighton, Laura Cronk, Iris Jamahl Dunkle, Anel I. Flores, Janet Jennerjohn, Kristen Kaszubowski, Ruth Ellen Kocher, Michele Kotler, Amy Lemmon, Michelle Otero, Bethany Price, Robin Reagler, Anna V. Q. Ross, Marion Wrenn, and Marina Hope Wilson; for Chryss Yost and David Starkey of Gunpowder Press for their care with this manuscript and for taking another chance on my work;

for our community of friends and family—from school to soccer to yoga— thank you for supporting us during our impossible year, and for helping us honor Austen. Gratefully, there are too many of you to thank;

for my spiritual teachers who continue to help me grow;

for my husband, Andy, and our children, Connor, Austen, and Celia.

This book is dedicated to my son, Austen, who left the body on August 3, 2023.

Austen, may your memory serve and heal others. Eighteen years were not enough, but I am eternally grateful that you chose me to be your mom. It was/is the greatest honor of my life. I love you beyond space and time, beyond the beyond.

About the Poet

Catherine Esposito Prescott is the author of *Accidental Garden* (Gunpowder Press, 2023), winner of the Barry Spacks Poetry Prize, *Maria Sings* (dancing girl press, 2017) and *The Living Ruin* (Finishing Line Press, 2012). A *Best of the Net*-nominated poet, her work has appeared widely in print, online literary journals, and anthologies. Prescott is the co-founder of the literary arts nonprofit organization SWWIM and the editor-in-chief of the online poem-a-day journal *SWWIM Every Day*. In addition to her work in poetry, Prescott teaches yoga philosophy and leads yoga and writing retreats. She lives with her family in Coconut Grove, Florida. See http://catherineespositoprescott.com

BARRY SPACKS POETRY PRIZE

Color Advisory Board, poems by Michele Santamaria *

Dear Empire, poems by Holly Karapetkova

Burial Fragments, poems by Keith Ekiss

In the Cathedral of My Undoing, poems by Kellam Ayres

Accidental Garden, poems by Catherine Esposito Prescott

Like All Light, poems by Todd Copeland

Curriculum, poems by Meghan Dunn

Drinking with O'Hara, poems by Glenn Freeman

The Ghosts of Lost Animals, poems by Michelle Bonczek Evory

Posthumous Noon, poems by Aaron Baker

Burning Down Disneyland, poems by Kurt Olsson

Instead of Sadness, poems by Catherine Abbey Hodges

DRYDEN-VREELAND BOOK PRIZE

Lung Hours, poems by Jessica Purdy *

Night Halves, poems by Christine Marshall *

Three-Day Weekend, poems by Christopher Blackman

ALTA CALIFORNIA CHAPBOOKS

Patrilineation, poems by Carlos Andrés Gómez *

Here, on this 76L, poems by Michelle Moncayo

Alba and Other Songs, poems by Fred Arroyo

The First Amelia, poems by Amelia Rodriguez

On Display, poems by Gabriel Ibarra

Sor Juana, poems by Florencia Milito

Levitations, poems by Nicholas Reiner

Grief Logic, poems by Crystal AC Salas

JOHN RIDLAND POETRY PRIZE

Figeater, poems by Andrea Carter

Sad Animal, poems by Joshua McKinney

CALIFORNIA POETS SERIES

Rosa Mundi, poems by Mary Ann McFadden *

In Praise of Late Wonder, poems by Lee Herrick

Downtime, poems by Gary Soto

Speech Crush, poems by Sandra McPherson

Our Music, poems by Dennis Schmitz

Gatherer's Alphabet, poems by Susan Kelly-DeWitt

—

Peculiar Fire: Tens Years of Gunpowder Press

Learning to Drown, poems by SM Stubbs

Empty Me Full, poems by Catherine Abbey Hodges

Frangible Operas, poems by Susan Kelly-DeWitt

Before Traveling to Alabama, poems by David Case

Mother Lode, poems by Peg Quinn

Raft of Days, poems by Catherine Abbey Hodges

Unfinished City, poems by Nan Cohen

Original Face, poems by Jim Peterson

Shaping Water, poems by Barry Spacks

The Tarnation of Faust, poems by David Case

Mouth & Fruit, poems by Chryss Yost

FULL CATALOG AVAILABLE THROUGH

GUNPOWDERPRESS.COM

* Indicates title forthcoming in 2026

www.ingramcontent.com/pod-product-compliance
Lightning Source LLC
Chambersburg PA
CBHW030500130626
46549CB00007B/2801